T0308630

The BOOK *of the* ANGEL

Medbh McGuckian

The BOOK
of the
ANGEL

Wake Forest University Press

Copyright © Medbh McGuckian
First North American edition published 2004

All rights reserved. For permission to reproduce or
broadcast these poems, write to:
Wake Forest University Press
Post Office Box 7333
Winston-Salem, NC 27109-7333

Printed in the United States of America
Library of Congress Catalogue Number 2004112242
ISBN (cloth) 1-930630-17-4
ISBN (paper) 1-930630-16-6

First published in Ireland by The Gallery Press
(Peter Fallon, Editor)

Contents

for Clare

The author wishes to acknowledge the inspirational friendship of the late Gregory Peck and his wife, Véronique, and family; also to thank the Librarian and staff in the library at Queen's University, Belfast.

And the voice which I heard from heaven spake unto me again, and said, Go and take the little book which is open in the hand of the angel which standeth upon the sea and upon the earth.
— Revelation, X, viii

PART ONE

The Publisher of Inwardness

This is the time after seasons.
It is too warm for spruce
to sketch a deep horizon.

I photograph asleep
like the detachable soul of a child
the final resting place of metals

in the receiving waters,
so mobile in soil,
by my wordwork,

by taking his lifetime
into my mouth as a word
to make a world.

A word that ends up under
sea-ice, or a parable
by the seashore embroidering dawn.

The Dream Theatre

First I drew in the air the roads
like clouds thrown further back
and a heart like the sky:

then, in the sand, composed
of tiny starlike fragments of coral,
your story, in pieces, as it is.

A story of dreaming, sleeping
with one side of your brain
in the italicized darkness

that roams the world imagining
a world without empire,
lost and dangerous as a dream.

❧

In the outline of your dream
you turn your head to the right,
but look to the left,

your mouth a little open as if
to bite, but never attacking thin air;
with real smiles changing its fine

structure, like the dreams
of a champion oyster, whose face
is then utterly forgotten.

❧

It had broken as it should have,
my sea-horse shaped memory,
the warm-blooded bowl of your sleep

without touching your brain,
building up its library
in its graveyard of dreams,

or your eight-day-old memories
that are paths into your dreams,
and your empty, high-quality waking.

∿

Until, note against note,
a dream comes on, and becomes
a place to live,

a dream-play in the open loop
of our dreams, now and equal,
white and coloured,

writing out the sleep debt,
a hundred minutes of dreaming,
underneath that late, inner star.

The Parents of Dreams

Shadow-freshness . . .
a stone boat races
on a sea of dust.

It seems divine
and winged
as a bird that shows itself
only twice;

or the antiworld
that surrounds the world
and sets a snare
in the path of the sun.

A new skin
rolling over the old earth,
the relatively slender walls
of its tawny skull.

The stones pressed
on the fields
are the furniture
of the earth.

The voice or talk
of the water
is of freedom
from field —

a countergift
of such dignity
anyone can judge
the vivid dream;

any technician
of the sacred,
knowing not all dreams
are truthful

and that heralded joy
can only follow
a dream's suffering.

What happened
happened for him
who wanted to dream
of all the leaves,

whose dream had become
a prey,
like any dream that causes
an illness,
a dream fast,
selected after dance-days,

or winter-night dances,
pushing away
the globe with the fire
of his foot.

Closed Bells

Frost hollows
small areas of leaf
in gardenless
margins.

Wounded by the thought
of nests expanding,
they inspire
devotion of a sort,

using this world
as if not
using it to the full,
a risky limbo.

Frost action
on the loose-fitting stones
and frost-broken rock
over-divides itself

and puts the spent hops
with their pinch
of old seed
off flowering.

Rust will devote itself
entirely to
that ringingly taut
and ample root,

though they will come
into flower
together
a close grey spring

if you study
your windswept window
carefully
bearing their colours in mind

that would find the move
too much
if they did not
answer to this blue

found between the bones:
movement towards
a touch, with two
five-nerved lips

reflexed to form a star,
or one indistinct nerve
erect and desirable
in your violet throat.

Poem without Words

The smallest bare twig still,
everywhere a foreboding of resurrection . . .

confined to the ghetto, yet secure
in the familiarity of the passing faces,
I had been afraid of its reckless
inner strength

and sought a geography
as architectural forms
migrated across the religious divide,

their cool tensions
and tinted responses
like waterborne pieces of sea.

My purse as full of patience
as Christ's open mouth
whose blue we both loved
rose up and fell

in the pictured moon with white edge,
old picture of the new spring,
ring with a moorish setting
or a heathenish dress.

I yielded the foreignness
of what I no longer possess
to the perfected nature
of its much-needed light,

and lay in wait
for the garden of its unpossessed places.

Four Voices without an Instrument

Another March month has come
to raise the temperature of the world,
a self-opening, clear, in mourning,
becoming light.

The northeast wind
reads the quarters of the sky
where the moon falls awake
into its own mouth
till day and night are equal.

There is no dust, no deluge.
The blue of the city has swollen
or returned to itself
in its dark ship
the reverberating sea.

Even the light, I thought,
like a bell in the air
already out of tune
through a slight snowfall,
would never be allowed its brightness.

Yet since we have been a conversation,
the three-in-one sign
of your stained-glass voice
has become my chosen one,
a garden surrounded by other gardens,
housing the seasons.

Though our lives may have overlapped
the musicians that blew out their candles
and left the stage, one by one,

now blow for me
a sunburst of winds
on their lowest strings;

so that not without wings,
when the mist vanishes,
the brightening, endangered earth
is the year's first angel.

Addressed to Fanny on Her Confirmation

Spring, the mortal temperament of dawn,
passes through here swiftly —
an ailing spring, more like a sob,
an error — a sorrow — a split key.

We are carried along in the adventure
as if within a missile.
In the sedimented violence,
the delectable statues of Christ,

crowning the city with angel-pure
mouths of youth, flee from its gardens
aflame at night. Then early perfume
that the muse like a docile bee

takes from the tenacious flower,
the everlasting fragrance
of the bud of a seasoning creature's
inability to become old,

suspends for an instant the laws
of love, whose high quiet
has proved too high.
The light grasps those few winged words

like worthless water, spreads
those three or four red-hot threads
too close to us, so that a walk
in any public place

is embittered by their unburnt bone,
and some divine nerve
of elongated turquoise
enters Berlin by the Rosenthal gate.

The Saints of April

This graced world,
two thirds of the way out
on a spiral arm,
appears to be without being,
fused in an atmosphere
like the court of miracles
in the bowed arch of my room,
in the stillness of my house.

Acres of time, unction and wheat,
painting spaces and crowds,
warm the walls to blossom-wielding sequences,
a lure for the next moment's
small amount of soul, shaking
but more erect. You used to like
cloudy days so much
in the discussion of day,

day that lied from within you
whenever there were words, attacking
whatever 'there' would mean,
uncaressed or perished co-redeemer.
But tenderness can also be this colour,
dry, alert and braided, speaking afresh
of that music a flock of nightingales
abandoned, this endless winter.

The Appearance on the Earth of Green

The sun grows, losing his face as a neighbour:
paired with light so low,
uplifted eyes see nothing
but tireless spotlights.

They capture the display
or interplay of the whole heaven
one might have inside one
like a harvester of managed forests

who builds almost bodily a mountain.
From the lake's point of view, such flow,
ground water becomes less transparent,
the marine sand will not be renewed,

as thousands of choked and lowered lakes
make a largely reborn landscape.
Bridleways suppressing the spring flood
cross low-herb meadows where a hundred

feet have walked. Frost-heave
in the surface soil means grass
gives way to bilberry, where streets
have begun to resemble young forests

supplying withered leaves
low-growing closest to the water
along extreme reaches of harnessed rivers
and land unprotected by snow.

Perhaps of all the town's residences,
the walls of a mediaeval fever chapel
will be the last to survive,
cut in four by fires and windthrow,

where an angel with a candlestick
keeps a christening bowl at his hip,
and Lucy, a *santina* in pink,
bears on a plate a harp seal's two eyes.

Armed Dance

I held in the same hand
male and female stones:
one blue variety giving
sweet light
like the sea close to shore;

and my increasing
certainty of touch
feared the virtue
of this weathered world
might be lost —

the personification
of the calm sea
and the soundful,
soul-tightening ocean,
might sever earth

from world,
though the god sealed them:
earth, the original ark,
holding his body
in its distant embrace,

the sky a prolongation,
and even an organ,
the colour of watered wine,
of earth missing water,
of his limping heart.

But it is not just any world,
despite the purposeless rain
these twelve April nights
ordered as from the grave's sky,
and the twenty-four winds

closing all available portals,
the eyelids and the intentions
of ships, so that the pulse
of nature can hardly
be counted.

And there is another world,
past the body thought
by the soul as its own,
her commonest garment:
past its near-bys

and far-offs,
like the seed of language
in this one,
the dark-brown
re-enchantment of his voice.

Rose Shoes

Different from every neighbour,
the mountain tries to enter the house
like the element in which the world swims.

Should we call this otherwise a creature,
showing its wear, its sojourn in the deep
yellow shadows the woman presses to her breast?

It is cored out, its shell of shadow,
which we have dared to call glory,
and brightly lit shoulder, outside of sleep,

a sky-blue gospel. The house turns
to control the seasons, part of the house
detains the falling evidence of light

and its daydreams; where my deepest
thought, which carries all thought,
falls through like a devotion.

Already the ignition of the skin
that he troubles and holds, touching
but not touching, is a desire that withdraws

from its satisfaction, from electricity's
unnerving ways . . . not absolutely unseen
but missed by sight, whose imperfect,

perfectible, high-speed, machine-eye
could not explain the feast he desired
of the absolute repose of the earth.

PART TWO

Studies for a Running Angel

She prolongs with words the growing fields
and, to make draperies, skies and clouds
on the larger arched surface,
or knots of gold cord on the ceiling
whose mouth would be tied shut,
the nude grey was often left
visible as tone. Did she build up
any depth of shadow, pushing away
the darkness of the universe
in its nearly seamless arrangement
around the six-lobed star,
with her arms and hands nearly closed
in a circle, like the month of May
with the nine muses, the integration
of sand unless of infinite beauty,
as is clear from your face?

1 *Chairé*

We will have to understand some such
word as 'today', a luminous Word
for the 'until' verse of the god-
making, brief Messianic stir
air-kissing the harmony of the data.

A time, and times, and half a time,
he half-miracles the night
three times its ordinary length,
then lifts a cloud that he is fond of
into his world at its dawn:

the goddess-shaped yearning
of a moon stained with clay,
unespoused and loosely embraced
in his left arm, swallowing a blade
of grass standing against the wind,

or finding a flower clinging to her
that she eats, a meditation
on two levels, an underground room
with a star that does not behave
astronomically —

the rest of the stars forming
a ring around it and the invented
birth. There are fourteen prayers
we should now say to the very different,
too lightly baptized limbs.

2 *A Chrisom Child*

All the old descriptions of the porch
remark on its blueness; the added twist
of the blue between the marble
and the meandering gold.

It is impossible to tell
from the brocade and feathers
of the robes, wings and hair of Gabriel,
from the tartan cloth of the angel,

whether he has already spoken.
The cushion plays such a very ambiguous
role, and the fall of his hair
may be compared to a crucifix

that previously disfigured the sky.
The wood, cherry, that within so short
a radius, carried death at its heart.
The young saint is weeping

at that view of the holy life
in his mind, like brown wallpaper,
and it is difficult to imagine
how his body fits together

in its heaviness and delicacy,
the underlying silver
of its conventional desire.
Cold still, his thin elbows,

and most extraordinary fingers,
the parchment of the border,
and the one quart of poppy water
re-shaping his head.

3 *My Carmelite Family*

It had taken me more than an hour
to come to life, under the rose-encrusted
influence of the star-driven morning.

A blue a bit too pastel, with all its accessories,
a colour he could not have given us
in a hundred years, familiar but shallow,

intense but guarded, multiplied the sensations
of his different flesh, though not
my ability to return the increased gaze.

Breathtakingly tactile, his beautiful
carnal mask distanced the white reserve
of the paper, yet brought it closer

to his cornerstones, the perfect control
of his hands' immense fresco about to move.
This eye reddened at his blood-red

accents and the pure indication
of his heart, belonging low, that owned
casts of my arms and feet.

So that the way we sat was a hearth
from which the layers emanated,
walking into the sea-coil of a song.

4 *A More*

The stairs begin with Jacob's Ladder.
They sit in each other's presence
in a room neither can stand up in;
they both have grey eyes.

The earth is spread out below them,
in small vanished areas of green vegetation,
wood sorrel, the herb alleluia, an earlier meadow
where they once stood fully upright.

She is caught with a breath half-taken,
holding a common rose and a pale book.
The pages of the book curl in space.

Her hands, incapable of gripping,
convincingly fold in a backward turn
against the standard furnishings, the bed.

The angel, from the behaviour of the cloth
in his waistband, seems to have no body
beneath his drapery: no feet appear below.

He carries forward his wing and arm
halfway between rising and sinking,
identified by the dove at his ear

which could be the severely damaged goldfinch
the Christ Child holds to his mouth
in the next stained-glass miracle.

What the simplified eyes experience deepest
in this pilgrimage church
whose beauty is strictly outward

is the candle-burned pearl on her head
like a triple head within solar rays,
her badly rubbed star-halo's
long association of vases,

the unfinished, leave-taking wings.

5 *The Angel Musician*

Crossroads tell it, to eyes begging
for sleep, how the bees flying
in and out of his berry-pink mouth
have vanished with other losses.

He lacks Gabriel's crown
of red and white roses,
successfully darkened into the garden
as she into her pale green chamber,

where she folds her arms inwards
for support, a dry tree behind her,
like a ghost in a burnt dress,
a living tree behind the angel.

The tree's pure hue may be a metaphor,
the landscape pulls the angel back,
the dove overlaps the tree
in a twisting movement,

building a tabernacle over the well,
and leaving strangely vertical
the lavender cushion, the margin
of raw wood at the worn-down windows.

6 *Modello*

A steeple when it is imperceptible for days
carries through the air a streak of blue
on the collar, and a sound other than singing,
a long answer like shadows that hush
in water.

She lay clothed, indefinite as the room,
or the green stair carpet woven
with yellow globes of the world;
and by the guidance of sunlight,
some blur in the misleading chandelier,

they conversed directly in bright daylight,
her hand overlapping his draped elbow,
as though a garden flowered foolishly
above the town houses, and the future
who left them in our keeping.

7 Red Angels

The sky suffers cloudmarks.
A patch of green lining
turned up over her foot
takes shade from the room.

Her timeless robe with its pomegranate
motif has a calmer fold pattern
than the escaped piece of veil
falling forward over her hair.

The red angels are sorrowing
at the nuptial meaning of her body
in their angelic time, the highest
taking a burning coal in his hand,

with intended highlights on his raised
arms and red collar, the lowest
holding a candle for the dying
with a coin, a curve in his sleeve.

All earthly things have died for her,
the silver choir lights in the porch
setting, the snowflake pattern
on the bedcover, in the bright stable.

8 *A Blessing Christ*

Only in the short time
when the light was annunciation-strong
would space be flattened out
to such a ravishing ivory.

Inhabitable world, near dormition,
that has not been fully realized,
as though the warhorse had
a moment before been reined in.

The corner itself is loosely marked
by the tree of sacroiliac joints,
a movement in, out and around,
a whorl at the edges of the field

like spirited handwriting
or a last judgement spread over two fields
of lyrical bronze. The stylized
earth requires the physical exertion

of two curtain-holding, censing angels
and the almost bitter power
of the interior springing of their ribs,
the distinction of their hands,

to reach the unflinching candour
of the direct gaze and perpendicular
glance the still-living Christ
directs across her criss-cross *stola*.

He has lost all rigidity
and rests his utterly relaxed arm
on her shoulder — no longer a Roman matron —
he touches Mary's crown.

9 *Saint Faith*

All in all, there were too many spires
and waves, more than my own footsteps.

The warmer-hearted sins wore blue
half-sleeves in the calm of the garden.

Summer stood nude, as alone as the rain,
her family smile absent, as many sleepless
eyes on her body as she has feathers.

I heard a roar of wings, a darker flesh,
and started walking, lest the mountain
should soar right out of the book,

then kneel down inwardly
over a holy organ such as a feather.

PART THREE

Garden Homage

Three windows are at work here, sophisticated
spaces against the day, against the light.
The sky looks as if it has been added later
to a glimpsed world as nobody saw it.

Small gaps of awkwardness between overlapping leaves
bring their time to us, as we our time
to them. The hand alone is amazing,
the skull and the owner's hand holding it,

together on a page for fifty years,
with the earliest smile. A rope vase
of flowers returns the angels
to the ground, that still beautiful brown.

Hand Reliquary, Ave Maria Lane

God knows that there is no proof
that part returns to wholeness
simply because miracles happen
at a single church-going.

Her verdant branches labelled
with the names of the five senses,
the garden not ours, she prayed
for her illness to last beyond the grave,

and be the unsealer of that tree.
She might have been dead for a week,
though she went on with her deep
dying, her womb a transparent crystal

turning into a brown relic
even before her death. The blinding
beauty of her hood opening
acted upon me as my own ghost

would do, sounding silk,
as with a lifting gesture
she tore off flesh from her hand,
driving wide her middle finger

into the palm of the other.
Till being a vessel, Christ appeared to her
as a dish filled with carved-up bread
so unnaturally sweet, so lightly crushed,

she could quench the tall language
of his image in her mouth,
which was the breast-wound, always on the point
of being taken, in his female side.

Celebration of the Name of St Philomena

Recognized by three successive Popes,
Gregory, Pius and Leo,
her feast was removed by splinter groups,
she was placed in the day of all martyrs,

but she was never uncanonized, a girl between
twelve and fifteen who had been beheaded,
not thrown to lions . . .

I offer you her spirit of gesture,
in an order moulded by desire,

her symbols, an anchor, an arrow,
and a palm,

all my land entanglements,
a bound cupid and a limp rose,

my green winter firing
its white winter tribute
up to the edge of your head's
bestarred winter, into its continent.

The Important Afterlife

He provided azure, steely
turquoise-mauve, changing grey-white,
grey-rose, grey-red that shimmers
still more by candlelight;

my narrator-angel, one foot
resting on her womb
in a wrenching meditation,
a sign that is placed in the first room.

The lowering of angels to the cross
with stars attached to cords
painted a new star over his head
like two pieces of heaven tied together.

Cape Fear Bank

for Candide

Old world upland garden
in the new world. A snake-rail fence
and a live hedge of blood-twig
planted by Brother Christ, Brother Lung
and Brother August. Painted (in 1824)
by Christian Daniel Welfare.

In the medical, or hops garden,
last year's parsley, opium poppies
that wandered, true citron,
scurvy grass, hyssop,
blessed thistle (or St Mary's thistle),
muskmelons, lungwort,
wormseed or old woman,
the cockscomb and the apothecary rose.

Rose campion, the Cherokee rose,
spider flowers and four o'clocks,
Angel's trumpet, Joseph's Coat,
Joe Pye weed and johnny jump-ups,
Lamb's Ear along with Bachelor
Button. Late peaches with Bishop's
early peas. Oxheart carrots,
wren's egg and Rob Roy beans.

Tennisball and lazy lettuces,
vegetable oysters and tree peonies.
Globe amaranth and tassel hyacinth.
The blackhaw, bitternut and sourwood.
The mockernut, the Carolina allspice
(having the fragrance of strawberries),
the serviceberry, the Carolina silverbell.

The river birch and river plum,
box elder and shortleaf pine,
the honey locust and the black
locust tree, winged elm,
fringetree, all the oaks,
swamp, scarlet, pin and post.
Lantana and bottle gourd
vining the lower pleasure grounds
where one of my bee stands
began to swarm . . .

According to the compass rose,
the furrow of the graveyard
uniquely is in blue,
and in Bethabara, house of passage,
an arbour of live cedars
had their tops chained together
into a green dome, had doors cut
through their branches
to grainfields of ancient spelt.

The Lily-grower

A truce to searching out the haunts
where lingers late the rose.
— Horace

This is the house of the faun,
and the villa of the mysteries.
It is the house of the ocean gods
and of the golden cupids,
the house of the silver wedding.

Its true garden is made to curve
with the shoreline of dwellings
in the sea. Pear matures on pear
on wondrous trees plundered after battles.
By every chair is a tiny fountain.

The demi-lune basin remains full
without overflowing. Throughout
the riding-ground can be heard
the sound of the streams directed into it.
Letters in flexible leaves spell out

the gardener's name. A pleasing
arc from the elaborate mouth of a mask
waters the upper walkways,
then the short sides of the garden
and the rounded turning-points,

sometimes the whole at once.
As doves will come to whitened walls
the fish in the long thin central pond
are fed by hand and come when called.
One cave does not admit the rays

of the sun, while the other keeps them
until the sun sets. The plan of the hours
resembles a pair of wings whose time
should be read by retracing steps.
The birds on the owl-fountain only sing

when the owl is looking away from them.
No shady foliage is more short-lived
than those soft-haired hyacinths where
a dark, heavily-built figure enters
the late garden, piercing through

the centre of each inward-turning flower —
the god of rust, like Tragedy, raised
on actor's boots, or the pine-cone which,
when other flowers' meaning fails,
even after a fire, has living scales.

A Lost Epistle to Sister Beatrice

What if I never crush your ladyskin
to open flight in a division of flesh,
or place the eddies of a train
hurled at the sea on your eyes?

For whom, as for you, was the gate of heaven
ever opened twice, now at the nape,
now at the brow as, rainbow by rainbow,
with a better star, the ice was tightened

round me? Their wings carry along
the starlings through the sinister
spirals of violence splintering all cities,
as if set down by every hunger in a field of wheat.

It is not far, by bird, plant and ghost,
to traverse the fullness of heaven,
the heaven that you journey through,
where the wine is tempered and fragrant

like your body, the imagery of your shoulder.
Provisional, radiant compulsion, your worth
is worthless, merely the twilight
whose threads of misshapen desire

have crystalized into act.
I have been together with this
accident of love, her stride,
her silence, her gestures of disdain,

and cursed the bread lost on her,
her all-out glorification,
her angelification. In the rhythm
of new dusks and new dawns,

I will re-call the first-heard muses
from their banishment, their real,
if narrow quiet, like stillness
in a living flame, which unwinters

itself in three melodies;
and tie their words together
in the screen of a sung conversation
like the poet of the afterlife

becoming the world's guest,
or the semblance of an angel
of the absurd overfaith
that somehow lets the year move on.

Eye with Clouds

A bough has crossed the moon-swept brilliance
like poured shade or wine spilt into sand;
I touched deeply along your letter
my cherished blue, holding it to the light
for the sake of lightness not visible to the eye.

The big long ponds, unfurled at heights,
renewed their sky, a horseless road
posed its cool, fair leaves, some fields
paled apple-yellow and savagely
stopped moaning.

The thin iron shutters
loosed an inner verdant space
between a second set of lower walls
where a second angel hovered.

And after this one half-a-grace,
a porous gloom, a dark sporran,
as though we were children dressed for snow.

Angel in Two Parts

How often, truly, have we found ourselves in that square
of the city by day, dressed against the chill,
watched by a faraway statue in the gloom
of the street with its cares and glances?

On the horizon a small black train enters the station,
a window flickers and lights up red,
and someone stops to look back or returns
our gaze with the same wan evenness.

It was here, more than anywhere,
that we met, the sky unfeathered and burned,
as if a valley were pounded into it,
the leaf that could be found fluttering

takes leave of the step. A train-ride outside
the city, end of the beaten track, end
of final roofs, beginning of trees however crooked,
the mountain makes a breast of its shoulders.

And before it dies this sort of mental year
will be multiplied five internal times,
before January leaves winter altogether,
if the world did not take this half a path.

Now one hears the words, now not:
they depart in the flame, intent upon
the first thunder. The last angel
sings the words, at first so dazzlingly severe.

The Heaven of Jupiter is nearly full, from the previous
Christmas; the year itself is a doorscreen
resting on the purple blood, but open therefore
in a special way. Even though it has time, still,

the mountain above the door is weatherless,
supplying time for time, till the angel-
boatman turns out to be the angel-
doorkeeper, pulling out with his bread the weightless keys.

The Soldier in Him

When our lips pray
I am craving for one speaking,
this shall, blue, front-ranking mist,
response in a mouth.

The wings of the gate
burned too low,
and quarter-real,
part of a world passed by,

a double was,
a river pouring blindly
step by step
to outdie itself

at the place of the glance.
Something vanished
with its lust for it,
only a single word in length,

the sunlike eye
torn open
to address the world
as a creature.

There begins again an hour
on the day that he is living
which shines not like a fountain
but a face, an eye,

a purified lip
that, when the searchlight
of his prayer withers,
no longer has any need to move.

Fallen God of Bone

The slight disquiet —
feeling the inside edge
of the prison of my body,
imagining that you were about to die . . .

at the end of your life,
turning round towards
meanings immediately lived,
admitting that it is a dream,

was a kind of everyday death
on this deserted earth,
the wave bleating
right up to your absence,

tracing that line of foam,
and drawn to those fringes
in the environs of your soul,
at the surface of your body.

I let myself be led
every second,
misunderstanding your desire
as an entire part of your body,

but I say at once
it leads to no harbour,
the fragmented avenues
of the landscape of sensation.

The self is much too real
and you had consecrated it
to silence, though you
keep silent in very different ways . . .

your gesture of separation
a gesture of overtaking
the very force and treachery
of the separation.

Evening recollection
of the day past,
in a night not soon
to be ended,

the night it denies
lights up the night
from inside, such as
she is, this evening.

You make the truth inside yourself
exactly the same type of light,
and a light seems to tear itself
away from your body and cross the room

where I encounter now my only
language, an eye that opens
at a summit, something prior
to the sentences we speak,

as if, in the eloquent
survival of that voice,
spirit said something
I wanted to say,

whose hand is not light enough,
whose touch is too long,
ever to name that strict absence
our interweaving.

The Night Birth

I think for a breath that you
invited my out-breath, warm from the throat,
like a cool well where the rain
did not stop once.

I saw you for weeks and months
though all was fleet,
and I hover and hover a few feet
from your storm-tight, last-time look,

never too far away,
and never too near,
which was the right, intangibly
radiant way to appear:

the ideal distance, a kind of ice
or really hollow glass
that tried hard to be born
as a due caress in clay.

For ten high days we burned
with the same fire the sun began
to help, and all my homages
greyed the ripeness about you

like a leaf's complexion browning
your indoors hand, and solving
without the person visited in view
what became of the light that you were carrying.

In the Ploughzone

To see the underworld as if it were this world,
but folded over,
my two soles touched another's body.
Traces of my leather sandals lay beneath
a cow-hide.

Ditch and pit and bridge and hearth
and step and pool and kiln.
The head on one bank, the body on the opposite,
with the child asleep on the divine
Easter of her breast.

Stream of milk on one cheek, stream
of blood on the other,
a white blow which leaves no mark
on the whites of the bed-linen;
but a blow with palm or fist which leaves

a swelling, a wound requiring a staunch,
is the uneasy red dye of a cloak,
the value of a cloak, the presence
of an oak-seedling, its leaves
in a chalice on the altar.

Its knotless netting passed around my body
twice, a honeysuckle rope
spinning a passable thread
from its bronze flesh-hook
towards an unseen sea-marking

denying, by oath of soul-death,
if the greater or lesser winds
will go ashore as charms
from which one dies feeling no pain,
the shrine remaining in the tree itself.

A Chaplinesque

The eyes painted on your eyelids
were false clouds, and yet instead
of burning the complete building inside you,
you let me walk around you
like a temple seen in its completeness.

The camera in your mind's eye
stood up to the weather of one who gazes
at an actor, wanting to be strong,
as when you stand in the middle of the threshing
floor, your voice surrounds you.

If the house might have a voice . . .
if the same door might represent
two places . . . why such a line of stones
might be there . . . The city turned itself
into a theatre, and acted itself out.

With maximum proximity, an isolated
close-up sufficiently long, so the savour
of the city was as close as the guards
against your lips' sweet edge, at nearly
grazing incidence, then shifted west

and north into converging eye-lines.
I imagined an off-stage, purified world,
a gold and ivory statue, clothed,
immobile, a body that is on fire,
a silver skeleton;

and felt unborn, my cries hidden
behind a wall of knitted roses,
pacific in my arrival as a moment
of grooming, just the opposite of forgetting,
found and inherited.

But you were leaning on your spear
in a display of exhaustion,
imprisoned within the cylinder
of the given play, from which,
by a sacred route,

a vista of both the performance
and the sacrifice, actor
and onlooker, you were slipping out
on no clear exit line,
passing from the sunlight to your home.

Gold Universe

I look across the teardrop universe
and see you flattened and slowed,
like stored wonder, or the effort
of the river to hide.

At daybreak you have a view
of the foothills it leaves unhighlighted,
chilled in the full current.

You are being held motionless near
a planet, and your study of angels,
the now fading apostles,
could hollow out the north

by its interpretation of haloes
as some limit of their beauty,
by the nutrient of friendship
in your first cherishing words.

Processes within that ship are unfolding
and after a decade or so of ship-time,
which does not look contracted,
like land-time, on the light's voyage,

you will have aged on your return
less than those who remained behind,
when the light overtakes you, a wave that passes
even through the spaces between the stars.

PART FOUR

Angel's Eye View of the Bridge of Sighs

*This photograph has a much more gentle feel,
the weather anything but serene, the green leaves
even higher, wavering along one edge.*

*Some unevenness in the sky, the last four days
of September meant that all the sun could do
was make the image of the window as visible as it ever
    would be.*

Sagrario

Some have in them the deluge
and not the ark; the agitation
of wingless angels throughout
the pathways of the world.

It is not the path which just happens,
the thought behind the onslaught
on breathing beings heavy or light,
love burning love in a new way of dying.

A gently swaying, slightly unstable rhythm
recycles the exact, spiralling pose
of the summer part of the temple,
when the rays of the moon began

to prepare the air to receive those
of the sun, and to decorate the sea
with an oscillating swarm of pointed wings,
the forty-two virtues which make the soul

safe for paradise. The rigid floor
became a mantle of supple fabric
climbing out of the streets,
a sky-clad jewel at each knot.

A field of giving and a fewness of wishes.
Each bird in thin casings
of crystal touched by sound
flies free from its broken casement,

making a good friend of a climbed
mountain. There is no actual need
of wilderness, a tiny patch of brown
earth and a few scattered pebbles

is the bed of a future street.
For all things, even these lapsing passions,
like tooled gold, are beautiful
through his placing.

'What shall my west hurt me?'
All but one of the seven joys
of the virgin fully awakened
in her extended, foreshortened hand.

The stream-enterer, reborn
more sensitive, in one of the many
heaven-worlds; the once-returner
and the non-returner, passing

and not re-passing that lowest
honey-coloured green
feeding hungry ghosts on the evening
and morning knowledge of the angels.

Recipe for Red

The slow absorption of ruin
into the wholeness of place,
with its flicker of dusky silver and bone black,

buildings within buildings,
brings shadow within dulled touch.

Clouds with their attached shadows
set the key for inwardness,
bright cloud behind dark cloud,

so that the praying eye may drop and ascend,
as they push back the air from the palaces,
freeing its pearly apricot and strident yellow

deeper than crocus paternosters
to green the strangely molten landscape.

Banks of windows on the canal
loom pale, particularly across water,
their fire-polish rupturing the surface
like rinse-waters in a mesh of darkness.

The world looks back as if just born
into colour, even a dead colour,
though all colours partake of earth,

as if it gathered its skin of clear glass
to step within colour like a lapping
or a sway in foliage,

to shape accents of enlivened blue
on silk and constant mountains:

the cheaper mid-blue of fields that have migrated
to where the light in the sky
may tell a different story,

bowing the veins like such a sky
letting shell gold shuttle mottling
in skeins wayward as the heartbeat
or the rich word for fingernail.

Sudden mists poise on the false edge
in swathes and pockets whose colour is lowly,
the humblest colour, the balance to green,

or milled white — a spirit colour
holding the world together, interlaced,
however dreamy. And one visible arc
that seems to share our incarnation
then and now traces the earthy rose.

Picasso's Windows

If the war lengthens
it claws the zones
and kneads the built-up area
of the boy's head, for a month or so;

if body enters body
we are invited to rearrange the stars,
the heavenscape of starsouls,
with hard patches of sound,

all the waters the earth could not suffer
in its smallest veins.
Nothing has ever flown
through this dresdenized air before,

not even a fallen angel
lying soulless, tearing his eyes away
from his blue martyrdom,
which leaves an eye nestling

in his two islands of hair,
and encourages the eye to rest there.
Almost exactly a year later,
the charcoaled azure, as if rubbed with ashes,

tracks every breath
of that heavy dose of blue
wherein he once made shadow.
With a hand he knows,

outstretched as a shade
of red pearls that never depart from circling,
he muffles his underlying colours
and the lilac of his arms

in minor eye movements
like leaf-beings between his fingers:
remembering the gradual journey
as the softest of sins —

a youthful ribbon, a ray of ink,
a glance at the outskirts of what nature is not,
the astronomical moment of overlap
at the table's corner

where the knee-to-knee gripped
transparent curtains
still harbour the glow
of his fingerprints.

Disciple, Foal and Christ

It was not necessary for the angels to speak;
they knew each other before they fell
to every earth.

The first and greatest of deceivers,
like a pearl on a white brow,
within the moon,

removed the ice from his face
and was a short time a forester
in the forest of tongues, or verbal paradise:

he came as a star-bent eagle,
in intensely personal form,
a limb of his soul touched down most musical
in a field being ploughed for the third time.

His words remain, as they descended,
wisdom beyond wisdom,
the roads on his breast,
the sieve of dark at his side.

PART FIVE

Moon Script

The garden incarnates as if doubled;
the wind settles in the two gardens;
the hushed garden ushers in that other time.

In the space between one shore and another,
one powder-blue, lemon-breasted bird
is barely moving water on a snowed field:

a border searching night's inner vision
for ghost words after trees fall.

Silva

The meaning of the wind has changed,
self-reeling energy, so musical,
so strange and perfumed, calling
one or two birds enough.

Old music, old sounds, our normal
tears, are swathed in the smoothness
inside and out of the bittersweet
laughter. Reaching out his body

to add change like this,
his awayness is a fire-coloured
countergift, his seven dying words
in twenty-five different languages.

Playing with Stars

Qual si lamenta perchè qui si moia
per viver colà su, non vide quive
lo rifrigerio dell'etterna ploia.
            — Dante, *Paradiso*

This change in the sky
which before was kindled by him alone,
by his rising on the shrine-map
like the early chime that wakes the monastery,
makes the harbour warm with its own blood.

So old a fast in me
for the last sweetness, the white sheen
of the planet scolds the greenery
of leaves chilled on a feverish brow
with hair so black, all hunger for news of it.

We can imagine him smiling,
and for his body would have no other bier
than twenty-four plants encircling the bare ground:
the gem did not wear its ribbon, eyes driven
with one impulse must close and open together.

(Whoso laments that we die here
to live above has not seen there
the refreshment from the eternal showers.)

The Tenth Muse

We must have the arabesque of plot in order to reach the end.

— Lorca

I saw the news of his death
written in white blood
on the grass of Galicia.
It was secret, it was virtuous,
the slight lift of the rib-cage,
the air's last curves
in blood's last rooms
where he performed his dying,
the delicate bridge.

Anything but remaining quietly
in the window, wide-awake,
where daybreak does not enter
and black sounds shake
the low yellow lemons of dawn.
I used to have a sea
where the waves understood each other;
his eyes were two dancing walls
that stirred the plains

and I saw no temple in them.
Deserted blue that has no history.
This sacrament is so difficult —
now they are washing his skin
in oil of white lilies and buttermilk,
eternal skin stopping the mirror
from mirroring.
The water in which his bones
have been washed sleeps for an hour.

And now, with a brief visit
to the cathedral, they bury

his waltzing ribbons in oiled silk,
and the softest pauses
of the veins in his body
that each loved in a different way.
The coolness of reeds swaying
nowhere reaches the dark apple
of his head, his night lying face up,

no blush, ashen-maned,
camellia to be grazed on,
as if a man could outlive
or out-travel his beauty
like gardens. I know very well
that they'll give me a sleeve
or a tie with all its omens
this cavalier winter:
but I'll find him in the offertory,

unbodied arrow in a city of wells,
water-voice the equal
of the Manhattan snow,
unaware that the world is alone
in the sky's other slopes.
What a burning angel turned
to ash I seek, a double
childhood, chameleon
whose branches built a nest!

Spells for the Embalmers

I believe that you left the heart in place,
fringed with locks of gold wire.

That the blue tissue of the hands
was separately wrapped
in beaded net.

That the unprepared harmony
of palm wine and cedar oil
pealed at the same moment.

And a flimsy, waxed sail
that grew more and more threadbare
looped so riverwise about
the alder brim,

moon-like blades unlocked
the daily bread window.

Street of Straw

Some six thousand miles away the sixth hour burns
and they prepare the candle for its flame,
a simple light, but parting all the tresses
of the flower's open spray, among the loved branches.

If Jupiter and Mars were birds and could exchange plumage
winter would have a month of unbroken day
and rain its rain like a reversed fall of snow
losing its mid-sky imprint in the deepening sun.

Time has its roots in that vessel, in the other its leaves,
and heaven has no other where than my place, my place,
my place, name it ten times, laden with angels,
sifted out and climbing with his eyes.

The Blue of Lullaby

This note has been stitched in
as the closing prayer of an old book
or eleven windows showing overnight
summer and winter to your inward rectangle
of house-shaped bark,
leaving nothing, if possible, in the dark.

Eighteen re-openings; eighteen ways
to be promised in advance;
the perfection of a day for colouring the moment
when you first fall asleep,
and with the braids of your black hair
they tie your hands.

Total theatre beneath the sand,
not a second late in making your entrance,
dressed in poetry and a crown of poppies
from your blood's path across a humble meadow
of strident green. Your breath comes
from far away, heart of a heartless world.

While with your spent pulse like a masked moon,
stripped to the waist and looking for itself,
you use your arms to suggest
moon-surface trees,
where doves black and sightless
breed further relics of the many eyes

which will imprison you.
Go to sleep, carnation,
the weight of your voice,
each decade that you were alive,
almost nothing, not a leaf,
in the blind glass of my breast.

Angel with Blue Wings

Though I understood, almost feature by feature,
the unity of a world in your soul,
if I prolonged the look
to rediscover your face,

you would make someone else passionate,
or even seek to disappoint
my quarter-smile in the claws
of a laughing look.

Oversoft your eye, your hand,
the heldness and stillness
of your seated step,
fingerprints and palmprints large
against a body felt as pale
in the first stages of resurrection.

Through a doorway hung with rags
the darkness of the room belongs
to the side of your body,
the depths of your body's darkness

its blindness and obliviousness
to being beheld in a locking of gazes,
so that the act of seeing comes to seem
almost beside the point.

I would no longer say anything to your eyes,
the school of your eyes, the eye of the dead
at that precise moment when mourning begins,
two eyes that I must get over mourning.

But where now is the heavy step
eaten out of your lungs,
just having left you,

your gaze's own will to come
clear of your body,

the intimacy which was born
of your flesh-pollen's willed roughness,

the left-over-right or masculine
buttoning of your jacket,

the feeling of that line of light
at the *profil perdu* of your fingertips?

Agnus

Dust is thrown up
by the working out of the thunderclouds,
the hundredfold 'I' of its limbs
breaking through the decayed barriers,
drawing three wordless lines.

Ghostlike voices
shooting down on trumpet beams
above the firmament
start the strings' ever-renewed
listening; the minstrel touches

the harp within the piano.
A loitering sun,
preferring the strangely hurried
autumn season,
leaves every morning

like a dayraven, returns
apparently stubbornly
in the evening to sit
on our shoulders
and tell us the news,

its overripe candles
warming the air
of the west-eastern divan.
I fold the night into you,
housed one,

unhoused one, the unforeseen
edge of prayer outside
your roomy-hearted
essence of all renaissance.

A Bed for Phoenix

Xenia, my guest-friend,
you are called Resurrection,
you are called Easter,
you are called Pentecost.

Like four masses going on at once,
though low and simple
and on lesser altars,

you masquerade as kinship,
many-stringed, your lip-muscles
carving out successive parishes.

Father-stranger, too-perfect
replica, when my illness
was the light from lamps
made from hollow lemons;

when the day was betrothed
to the coming blindness,
laying by the name
of the year's year;

you breathed on the water
three times, and the site remained
springlike throughout the year.

When the world of the dead
was swollen by an oceanic
distance, by my sleeves
of metal tight enough
to seal off the air,

the grooves inside each bone's
loneliness lapped with thread

were a seating for the flat
of your fingers.

Using wood from the nettle-tree,
and the Greek word for actor,
the answerer, the respondent,

using a region of your lips
on each side less supple,
or less sensitive, you made

your thistle-shaped mouthpiece
cover the whole reed
and the whole upper bulb.

The Angels were a Mistake

The cruelty blossoms,
two halves of a now
sent through time
as owls are known to fly headfirst
into the walls of barns.

I see that his name
is contained in yours,
and often think of you
as a pilgrim before a distant shrine,
violated beneath archways.

There is more sky up here,
there is more earth,
and everything moves from the trees
to ensure the earthiness of the heart,
speaking directly over the wound.

His mouth within centimetres,
and his night-painting hat
with its halo of candles,
he garners the only deep blue
to avoid the blue in the sky

bearing the shed radiance.
The look of grace
burns down to a yes-no
at the rim, a fold-over
of white garment at the sternum;

pain sowed and pain reaped,
an ellipse of flesh that has dispensed
with the sheen,
a stippled swan to show him
anchored at the height of his glory.

Charcoal Angel

A moonlit night a hundred years ago:
proximity to a shore, the desired scenery,
the desired night.

Sky as hard as a wall.
Sea drowned in the sand.

Two knowledges, one face upon another,
newly created rose, though the sea-forms
in a squall are not repeated:
he has too much moss upon his temples.

Absence of pupils, but he has eyes
in his voice, that scarred voice
that seemed so near, it's by his voice,
it's in his voice that he dies.

We speak around it, as if it were wandering
along the rim of the wound's old hours:

yesterday, a strong wind blew away
the ivory inscription and the flowers.

Soul Being Saved by an Angel

Some of the blessed turn to look down
from within a cocoon shot with blue
at free-floating souls fished up to heaven,
past the descending vices.

Two have ceased to sound their trumpets
as Christ's eyelids, the tinder of grace,
scrape back the small corrections
to the cleared sky, the way into the year.

Unengaged with other psyches,
the green-filleted angel
who digs his feet and knees
into a stair-stepped cloud

crushes against the billowing shroud
that seems the discarded companion
of a climbing, lavender-draped soul
hurried out of the chapel.

Vision of a Soul's Release from Purgatory

One turn of the bared heart
in whom the heartbeats could be felt
very near, this second heart
had to wait for birds to arrive
at the speed of blood in their multicoiling

to know in all the angles of the wing in flight
the slightest stirrings
of the suddenly illuminated body,
its final melodic curve,
always and all along opened out,

if prayer did not bend
the lightness of your dying.

Poem Rhyming in 'J'

The spaces of my blaming soul
were a half-shell of branches, or a rose
of wish, where birds killed themselves
between my eye and its lid.

Touch after touch of pure surfaceness,
the pressure of hand on lap,
the exitlessness from the city much changed
and constantly changing.

I had a way of beginning
like the presence of morning light,
not true morning, in my chanced-upon images,
turned in the hand like votive wax

offering the body whole, to the author of twilights.
I veiled him with my hand from both worlds,
till one third of the night was over,
and the months appeared in human form,

safe passage across that wasted summer,
to fix the destinies for the coming year.
How accidental, your kindest kiss,
the nightingale of your tongue

exactly on a heart like dust, like soil,
with its ruse of affliction as its door.
Words remain on the shore, but when the angel
falls in love, with his different prayer movements,

he is the perfect human.

"If mid-nineteenth-century society had allowed for a female Edgar Allen Poe, how can we know that she would not have written that the death of a beautiful man is, unquestionably, the most poetical topic in the world?"

Lisa Dowling, *Desiring the Dead*